Leone's Little Book of 'Love, Life and Poetry

Leone H Williams

Copyright © 2022 Leone H Williams

All rights reserved.

ISBN: 9798806866432

DEDICATION

To my Children – Tish, Neil, Chasteine, Najii, and my sister Vivette who each shared my journey and struggles at different stages in my life.

CONTENTS

	Acknowledgments	i
	About the Writer	ii
1	**Love's Journey**	1

Where is the love?

The Card

All These years

Burning Desire

Strange Encounter

Heart Break

Hooked

Awakening love

If you knew

Is it possible

Flipping Heart

How Can You?

Many Times

My Love

Me and love

My Heart

My Word

Pain

Self-Search

Time Stood Still

Tragedy

Why

Who Are You?

Did you love me then?

Did He?

Silent Man

2   Life as I see it   37

I am a poet

Lone Mother

Beauty

Disturbance

Hunger

Insane

Lazy Girl

Life

Loneliness

The Day My Father Died

The Mind

The Poor Man

The President

Almost Waisted

Freedom

The clinic Scene

3   Jamaican Patois (Patwa)   56

Ganja Baby

Gilbert 88

Heads a government

Lazy Bwoy

Jamaica Bus Runnings

Mad Man

Mi come a London

Life eena Ingland

4 Prose   67

I am The Story

The child in me

Moving Here

5 Faith   71

Pleading Heart

My Prayer

Loving You Lord

The Almighty Father

ACKNOWLEDGMENTS

I want to say A big 'thank you' to my husband Michael who has supported me a great deal in the arrangement of this little book, who encouraged me to put it out there, when I was in the valley of procrastination.

I also want to thank these two main characters, whom because of their (mis) treatment of me, gave me the inspiration to write most of the love poems; my ex-husband Carlton Williams, who is still very much alive and Anthony Richards (now deceased), so good things can arise out of a bad situation.

About the Writer

My name is Leone Williams, formerly known as Leone West. I lived in Jamaica up until the time I moved to the UK in May 2000.

I have been living in Colchester England for the past 11 years; having lived in Birmingham for 11 years previously. I am married, the mother of four adult children, 2 girls, two boys; two of which reside in the United States. The other two live in England, one of which still is at home with me. I have had a few poems published before in a selected group of writers, a group that I was a part of many years ago in Birmingham.

I must admit I had become very dormant in my writing, it's what I call 'Chronic writer's Block'. I have become distracted by many events that took place over the years, of which some are still very active, so I haven't been giving the keyboard a lot of attention. I'm taking this opportunity to put these out and hope that anyone who reads them will both enjoy and identify with what was going through my mind at the time, especially the ones about 'LOVE'.

I have been writing poetry from I was around 21-22 years of age; In fact, it happened quite by accident. I got married when I was 19 and in the space of two years my ex-husband started playing the field, our relationship became strained and almost non communicative. He had gone back to work one Monday morning after a very strange weekend, I knew there was something wrong, but I didn't know to fix it. My thoughts were all over the place. I sat on my bed with my chin in my hands and suddenly, words started coming into my head. I got myself some writing paper and started writing. The words just flowed on the paper, and I realised I was just writing about how I felt; hence the poem ('Where is The Love?') materialised. The others are all related to something or someone that seemed significant at that time in my life, whatever or however they make you feel, I hope that they may make a connection and identify with you personally.

Leone H Williams, Colchester, England; April 2022

1

CHAPTER 1

LOVE'S JOURNEY

My journey through love, discovering it, trying to keep it, and losing it.

[Having a bad relationship can be devastating, it breaks you down and makes you question yourself, some of us even take the blame for the breakdown and all the terrible things that happens during the relationship.

[My first poem was inspired by the worthlessness, inadequacy and inferiority I was feeling; and so it became the norm to write out my thoughts as they happen. I then got to realise that using that method, was my coping mechanism; so many of my poems are based on real heartfelt pain, accompanied by the emotional turmoil I was feeling.]

Where Is the Love?

Why have we become such unloving, unresponsive, and
unfriendly people to one another?
Why is all this happening?
How far have we strayed from the beginning?
Where oh where is the love?

What is the purpose of our lives together?
Without the real true love, we once had.
Or was it just an impulsive infatuation that's really gone bad?
Where oh where is the love?

Why is our innermost self so hard to reach?
And yet, sometimes we almost make believe we have found
peace.
Then like the suddenness of rain, comes the grief, misery, and
pain.
Where oh where is the love?

Yet down in the depth of our hearts, there's a love so true
we'd like to impart,
but the skies are grey, and the earth is black,
and we never really stop to think about that.
Where oh where is the love?

Instead, with mouths entwined in words of wrath, we haste to
end and hurry to depart,
from that which and could have been, the only worthwhile
thing to be in:
"Love." Oh yes, love can be found.

The Card

I needed the ride, had places to go.
I could walk but it would be too slow.
Put out my hand to the oncoming van, blinking red.
He stepped on the brakes, nodded his head "come round the
other side he said."

In the leathery hardened seat, I sat.
We chatted and laughed about this and that.
We certainly didn't talk about yaad!
So why did he have to give me that card?

He seemed nice and smiled a lot.
I liked his shape, he wasn't fat.
Took sly, stealthy looks at him.
In my estimation he was trim.

With hands on the wheels his back seemed broad.
But why, oh why did I take that card?
I stepped down, smiled and said, "thank you" in the sweetest
way.
Thought that would be a nice way to end the day.

He held out his hand with something white.
I could see it plain, in broad daylight.
I could say no but didn't want to seem hard.
Instead, I willingly took that card.

It started then, right there in fine print.
Didn't understand, couldn't take a hint,
that on that card my destiny was revealed.
And unto this day my fate is sealed.

All These Years

I've lain in bed fretting, crying, wishing I was dead with thoughts of only you in my head........all these years.

I've planned, I've dreamed, I've worked it out so many times of things I'd like to do, with no one else but you........all these years.

I live to love you, share with you, proclaim all my love so true, enclosed you in my heart, swear on my life we'll never part........all these years.

I've imagined myself flying to the clouds and back, peeking in the future, looking to see if we're there together....... all these years.

I've looked around at times with a frown, to see if anyone else was there to be found but all I see is you.......all these years.

You've touched my heart in secret places, my love has grown and, in all cases, all I want to do is to love you.......all these years.

So now you ask; "WILL YOU BE MINE?" And I say "YES" for I deserved and believed I was getting the very best.......as it should be:

But oh, how wrong can one be?

Burning Desire

The emotional fluttering and thumping of my heart
Coupled with the vast space of that keep us apart
lead me to only one conclusion,
that love can only be compared to God above.

It is so real and true,
the things I feel for you.
The pulsating movement in my veins,
is a constant reminder of a prisoner of love in chains.

So vivid is your endearing countenance in my mind,
reminding me of the splendour I've yet to find.
Loving you, needing you, you've intoxicated my being,
knowing I'll accept no other is clearly to be seen.

Will this loathsome distance cause me to ignite and explode?
Or must I console myself with these visions untold?
Oh, very soon I hope my love I will share,
with you my heart's dream, so unique and rare.

Strange Encounter

So strange, exciting, and wonderfully nice; was our encounter.
Seeing you standing there silhouetted against all.
Not knowing who you were, or where you were going.
In the distance you were like a dream come through, I was me;
you were you.

Strange though it seemed, you answered all my silent
questions. When you smiled; I knew our meeting was no
accident. Our immediate and pleasant attraction was too
evident. You were there, I was there, it was done!

So long I've waited to see this day,
for someone like you to come my way.
You entered so quietly, like a beam of sunlight streaming
through a broken window, embracing me with all your charm
and magnificent grandeur.

Such an encounter is one I'll adore.
One I will treasure you can be sure.
For this is the day my dream has come through,
and it couldn't be done without someone like you.

Heart break.

I knew you'd break my heart again
It wasn't a matter of how, it was when.
How gullible and fool could I have been?
Couldn't see what I was letting in.

The sorrow and pain I'd long forgotten
Have now come back to drive me rotten,
You swooped in and let on all the charm
And yes, in the nights you did keep me warm.

You swore this time to be true and real
And yes, sometimes I almost did feel,
That on your part the effort was made
But with not much there, it had to fade.

I wish I could say I feel the same
But to me loving you was never a game,
Now I'm left again with a hole in my heart
For now, once more we've gone apart.

Hooked

My sweet, oh how I love you so.
It's such a shame, I'll have to go.
You don't need me, and that I do believe.
I think you'll be happy to see me leave.

In times to come you'll realise what you did.
Why all the love I sought, you hid.
If only you'd let me see, by just showing
care and concern for me.

I'm searching for a new love now.
Though one I know I'll find hard to keep.
Because in my heart there was only one.
And it was for you, it really went deep.

You made me cry; I really was sad.
I wanted to die; I was never glad.
My hope was for us to go on forever.
You've pushed me away and now it's over.

Awakening Love

I feel some things I'd thought I'd lost
they're growing strong and very fast.
You've woken me up, showed me the light,
it's a sensation of pure delight.

You've touched my heart in many ways,
it happened so fast in… just days.
I'm looking ahead, it's clearer now,
you've given me hope I've broken my vow.

you've done it!! Great man you are!
With arms outstretched and door ajar
upon your chest I'll lay my head,
and let you lead me straight to bed.

If You Knew

What would you do if you knew I was insanely in love with
you?
I guess you'd panic, try to deny it, or just simply wouldn't want
to hear it.

If you knew how much I cared with all my heart,
no feelings spared, for you I lived,
my heart gave space to no other in the human race.

Knowing you as I do, would sure slay you if you knew,
that deep within my being I cried, and for you to many I've
lied.

If things could be as, it was then, I'd sure pursue those trails
again,
maybe somehow for me you'd do things you now know, but
never knew.

Is It Possible?

Could it be that this has shown us the way to divine love?
So dear so passionate and delicately pure?
Like dew on the green fresh grass, opens the mind to wonder
and ponder.

Is it possible?

Can this thrive to the height of perfection no human has ever
known?
With mind, heart and body, combining all,
withholding nothing, consuming everything.

Is it possible?

Will it then be right to hesitate and prolong the unknown yet
vivid?
Emotions uncontrollable, restraint yet inevitable,
stupid of me then to ask.

Is it possible?

Flipping Heart

I wish I could tell my heart to stop doing these silly things,
but I know these are the emotions that true, divine love
brings.

Like skipping a beat here and there, thumping and rumbling,
as if to burst inside my chest.
Every time I think of you, I desperately want to
hold you, caress you and lay my head upon your breast.

I'm only a natural, simple woman, with supernatural feelings
for the man I desire day after day,
who makes me feel complete, safe, secure, and sweet in every
way.

If I could have just one wish before I die,
it would be to tell you; that loving you is like achieving the
stars, the moon and sky.

Then I could say in my last conscious moments; love has
found its way to the core of my being.
You've satisfied my yearnings and have fulfilled my dreams.

So, flip on my heart, keep doing your merry little dance,
you've done your part. You've stirred me, invigorated, and
fulfilled me, you make me want to jump and prance.

How Can You?

How can you say you love; and then inflict pain upon the one
most dear to you?
How can you say you adore, respect and care.
when you're never ever there?

It's happening to me, I am proof, so I can tell you why.
I've done and said everything I can, but you never, seem to try.

I can tolerate the snow; I appreciate the rain,
but don't do very well when it comes to pain.

So, think again before you say the words 'I love you'.
Because my heart has been affected a long time ago; and this I
thought you knew.

You can't fake love, it's got its own language,
it's silent, it's loud and full of action; it's something you do,
and in my book, it always works better with two.

Many Times'

So many times'…I've waited, hoped and craved to have you by my side.

So many times'…I've touched you with my mind, my spirit, my love, my being.

So many times'…I've wished you were here to hold me… just to hold me.

So many times'…The girl in me just want to reach out, and find the boy in you, to see if our love started then, if not then, when?

So many times'…I've cursed myself for nearly losing you, when all the times I couldn't see that you loved me too.

So many times'…I lie in agony just wanting you, with my entire body on fire for your love.

So many times'…I wished we could just be alone to explore, find and create the greatest love on earth, and call it our own.

So many times'…I wished we'd come together earlier in my life, wished you were my husband, and I your wife.

So many times'…I pray we'll never grow old, so we'd have each other till the end of time…So many times…

My Love

My love you mean so much to me, my heart hurts. I can't contain,
I have to tell you how much you're really worth!

You're conservative, you're sweet and shy.
I love you and those are the reasons why.

You're so different, you're almost not real,
your inner strength and power is something I can feel.

If the chance should come to show you just how much I really care,
hope it'll never be taken lightly, for the kind I have is rare.

Each beat of my heart spells your name,
every day every night it's always the same.

You live within me of this I'm sure,
for the love you give keeps me crying out for more.

Me and Love

I'm pining I'm crying; my heart is sure dying,
for the love I have gained and the love I have missed,
for the love I have yearned for and cannot resist.

It's in the air, it's in my sleep,
it's in my mind and ever so deep,
your smiling face, your act of grace,
your tender touch I can't erase.

Love clearly speaks so soft to me
of things I know in you I see,
you're steady always ready,
a little heady but most of all you're my teddy.

I say it loud I say it clear,
 whenever you need me, I'll always be there,
be it in the rain or be it shine,
I know I'm yours then, are you mine?

My Heart

My heart is jumping, skipping, thumping inside,
beating with a new rhythm unknown to me.
When I think of love and bygone days, indulging in long
forgotten scenes,
imagination and dreams.

My internal emotions can no longer lay dormant.
They're raging, kicking, searching for an escape route which
only my heart can provide,
So, it dances, it gurgles and bubbles with the joy of anticipation
inside.

Too long! Too long! My heart shouts
Why have you left me to die alone in darkness?
Wake up and attend to my needs! I need to love and be loved,
let my substance run, unscrew my valves, and let me flow again.

This heart of mine; it asks me questions I have no answers for,
it also tells me things I did not know before.
It counsels me, it contradicts and restrains me; but most of all
it beats to let me know I am still alive, and with it, the hope of
finding that fulfilling love it so truly deserves.

Pain

This agony, this turmoil, this excruciating pain I feel.
From deep within my bowels, a pain that knows no bound
And will not let me be.

It comes, it goes, it comes to stay, at home, at last to rest
It heaves, it shoves, it whirls
And yes, it settles inside my breast.

Oh, pain relieve me, ease me, I need my freedom now.
Ask of me anything; for peace you know I'll give
As long as you will go.

Pain, how long you'll last, I do not know, I find it hard to say.
I really think you've come to live
Until my dying day.

Self-Search

I looked within myself today and found out something new.
That I have never loved before, the way that I love you.

It's an everlasting feeling that grows within my heart.
An emotion that makes me wish we'll never grow apart.

I've never felt it before, that means it must be new.
I've only just discovered it, since I met you.
It's wonderful, it's sweet, and I want it to last my whole life
through.

Time Stood Still

Time stood still when I lost him.
For me my time on earth had ended.
He took my soul, my thoughts my spirit.
I didn't want to live, to go on, to continue my sad life on earth.

He was the centre of my world, the fulfilment of my dreams.
I believed in him I supported him.
He was all I needed.
For me he could do no wrong…because I loved him.

He woke up one morning and said, "honey I'm leaving",
"leaving where?" I asked.
"Leaving you" he said "I've had enough" then he was gone.
Disappeared as if we never met.
As if we never loved.

My heart was multiplied in tiny pieces.
I lived in a daze like a recluse who longed for death.
He was gone. I was nothing. No one wanted me.
I wanted no one…but him.

Yeah, he has returned, he has found his way back to stay.
Ask me why I let him?
He is the man I love.
Is there a better reason?

Tragedy

What tragedy, what pain?
When broken heart is survived only by agony and tears,
a heart dying slowly, shrinking in a body too feeble to hold it.

What tragedy what pain?

It's an effort to smile, wave a hand here and there,
to the unknowing, not knowing that you are wasting inside,
not seeing visual signs of neglect, reject and unreturned love.

What tragedy, what pain?

For someone whose love you thought you'd gained,
but only kept losing again and again.
It suffocates the mind, confuses the soul
and the pain keeps getting new while you're getting old.

What tragedy, what pain?

Why?

Why does my heart feel so, as if it's on a leap?
And what are these funny little feelings that's causing me not
to sleep?

Is it me or is it you, that's causing all this pain?
Will I ever see the sun again, or will it only rain?

You came and brought joy, but only for a while.
You put me up, then take me down and take away my smile.

I want to shout! I want to scream,
but most of all it seems; that all I need is just your love.

Or should I only dream?

Who Are You?

He said things to melt my heart, "My darling I want you, we'll never part."
He'd repeat himself a thousand times. Telling me how much he wants to be mine.

Who are you?

"I want you so much, I'm in pain", he'd say. "I can give you everything you need, please stay."
He'd put up a front, pretend to be someone he was not. Quoting to me all the money he'd got.

Who are you?

I was in the valley of depression; desperately needed a shoulder to lean on. He sounded real; he came on strong, "Just hold out" he said, "it won't be long."

Who are you?

It's all done now; it was never to be. I opened my eyes and behold! I see.
It was all words, so empty and dry. I think about it, sometimes I cry.

Who was he?

Did He?

He sat there reading, writing, or probably just staring,
rarely he looked up and when he did,
so intent and daring. With head raised a slight smile
followed, it must be my imagination. No! Of course, he
looked.

Or did he?

Not a word spoken, his shoulders erect and even,
only the flick of pen and paper sending off that familiar
sound, again and again.
Eyelids twitching, fingers trembling, oh yes, he moved!

Or did he?

One look said it all, momentary though it was.
There was a message, I saw it, it was directed to me.
I did understand though not a word was said, something was
going on inside of his head.
I could swear I heard him whisper.

Or did he?

Heart break.

I knew you'd break my heart again
It wasn't a matter of how, it was when.
How gullible and fool could I have been?
Couldn't see what I was letting in.

The sorrow and pain I'd long forgotten
Have now come back to drive me rotten,
You swooped in and let on all the charm
And yes, in the nights you did keep me warm.

You swore this time to be true and real
And yes, sometimes I almost did feel,
That on your part the effort was made
But with not much there, it had to fade.

I wish I could say I feel the same
But to me loving you was never a game,
Now I'm left again with a hole in my heart
For now, once more we've gone apart.

Silent Man

Silent man, oh silent man who sits alone, so alone in silence and solitude, with thoughts invaded only to eat and rest. You've turned your thoughts into images and projected them on canvas, with undeciphered patterns unknown even unto yourself.

Silent man, oh silent man with your deep, dark, unpenetrated emotions jumping to life before your eyes, let the swift dash of your brush interpret and unscramble the meaning of your dreams. Sitting astride your easel and canvas with brush in hand, like a weapon poised and ready for war, inflicting your mental picture into being.

Silent man oh silent man, with a million voices in your head, create and re-create them, bring each one to speak your unspoken wishes. Let your inner soul reach out, give your brush the power it seeks and the colour to express. Let your picture dance! jump! and scream without the use of words.

Silent man, oh silent man like an angered lion moving towards his prey, unleash that long dormant fire, that hidden power that resides in you, say it! sing it! shout it! Use that magnetic energy you possess to empower your brush as you dabble in paint.

Sound it from the roof tops! "I am the ever-silent man, but my picture speaks"!

Did you love me then?

When I turned to you because I thought you cared, seeking comfort for my swollen, aching heart, the friend I thought I'd found? Instead, you pushed me, shoved me, burrowed me into the ground?

Did u love me then?

When I searched for you, waited for you, fretted for you, when I watched traffic, counted the endless cars just to see you pass by. Got into agitated excitement when I saw you coming in only to be frowned on, looked upon with pity and indifference.

Did you love me then?

You never knew those long years back how my heart burned with bittersweet love, willing you to see me for who I was (not what you wished,) that I could desire a love so filled with resentment, so self-possessed, always ready to take but none to give.

Did you love me then?

While your child I carried in my womb, feeling him move, reminding me of those hot steamy nights spent with our raging emotions mixed with passion, sending you to sleep but kept me awake, wanting to tell you how much I wanted you but never did for fear of rejection.

Did you love me then?

When alone, jobless, pregnant and under your roof you thoughtlessly sent tremors up my spine with threats of eviction, implying that I walk the streets and beg with bags in my hand, your child in my body and memories in my head.

Did you love me then?

While in labor I cried but could not call your name, knowing that you did not care. "The Child" you called him as if he was a refugee, nothing at all to do with you, only me. In your perfect image he was born craving love, luckily, I had enough to give.

Did you love me then?

When in your tangled, tormented memories of passion you returned to find me eager, loving you still. After years of reject and abandon, you feigned surprised to see your son greeting you with warmth and an innocent smile upon his face, knowing nothing of the past. I know it, you know it, so this I need to know,

Did you ever love me at all?

CHAPTER 2

LIFE AS I SEE IT

Lone Mother

Noisy! energetic and rude busybodies; never seem to tire, seldom still, babies.

Vaguely aware of mother's exhausted efforts to guide and control, running!
Screaming! Jumping! Crying! It's a picture to behold!

Daddy! Daddy! is most often the cry, known to some of them as a part of speech, picked up going by. Lonely mother cried in pain as she gave birth; was father there? To stand by, show her love as tearfully his son she bears?

Yet with absent father carried on mother of human creation, for she was and always will be known as first of 'ALL' generations. Loving, gentle and kind, mother a child bearer, never ceases to care as each one gets dearer.

Though needing of love, tenderness and warmth, hunger may strike, and desperately in want, mother's unfailing love for her child though intolerable be, is substitute enough for the man she may never see.

Mother so pleasant, tireless and bright is often kept up with ailing child during the night. Never complaining though may never be rewarded, will never let her little one go unattended, unguarded.

Mother will go and mother will come, one thing is certain she'll never be lonesome; for the children she raised year after year, when fathers have gone will always be there.

Loneliness

Loneliness is a sickness; it eats your life away.
It's like a disease that cannot be cured, if given the chance to stay.
Loneliness is incomparable to all the feelings I've ever known.
The real effect is not realised until you're truly left alone.

There are different types of loneliness that's not easily recognised,
some manage to keep it securely, hidden, under a fake disguise.
There's the one you feel when your loved one dies, which is accompanied by pain, and there's the one you feel when your lover leaves, knowing you'll never see them again.

People get lonely for simple things, like; for just missing a friend,
some just don't want to accept the fact, that even friendships end.
The worst kind of loneliness I believe, is being lonely within oneself,
the hurting, inexpressible kind, that only you can, feel, and no one else.

Hunger

Hunger is feeling gigantic spasms of empty spaces in your
stomach with nothing to fill it.

Hunger is seeing someone eat and smelling the delicious
aroma of food but having too much pride to beg.

Hunger is passing a restaurant, seeing people dining at tables,
hearing the laughter, the clatter of plates and glasses and
knowing you cannot go in.

Hunger is looking out the window of a bus seeing the dirty,
unkempt homeless people digging in the garbage for
something to eat, knowing they'll find nothing.

Hunger is looking across your neighbour's fence seeing the
ripe mangoes, bananas and apples knowing if you climb over,
you'll be caught.

Hunger is being deprived of the chance to survive as an
ordinary human being by being able to eat; but eat what?

Disturbance

Madness, sadness, badness which one is it?
Feel it, see it, know it, only you can tell it.

The vibes, the times, it's a race almost a
disgrace, moving, shuffling boring through,
causing disturbance whatever you do.

The lowly, the poorly the rich and the great
have come together to celebrate hate.

No love around, cannot abound, certainly
in this time will never be found.

Beauty

Beauty is often looked upon as an outside feature, we fail to see and refuse to believe that it goes much deeper.

Assessing beauty is not seen in garments or the way we attire, it is neither seen in the style of gait or the way one aspires.

Beauty goes all the way down to the core of the heart, it's seen in the way you treat your fellowmen, in the love you impart.

Beautiful is descriptive of a person, whether great or small, as long as he or she genuinely cares for one and all.

Insane

Demented, mad crazy, insane put them together, they're all
the same.
Wise independent, sensible people who've lost control, now
possessed with evil.

Completely ignorant and left all alone, have now proceeded in
a world of their own, not caring for life, for family or friends
their only concern is for food to defend.

Everywhere that you go you see them stand by, on the street
side, in the corners, looking up in the sky. Some naked, some
clothed just drifting around, some bending, some sitting,
some lying on the ground.

They're out of their senses they're not in this world, good
men and women sometimes boy or girl. It pains my heart; I
pray all the time but what can I do? They're out of their
minds.

Life

Life is a two-way street as they say, but to me it seems like
three.
Because if there's a roadblock on one street and war on the
other, you may have to climb a tree.

The love we feel for another is compared to that.
Because you hate them and then you love them.
Next you try to rearrange them.

It's funny how men say 'I hate you' then get into bed with
you.
'I love you', then show you the door.
How can we please them? That's a question for sure.

Men and women differ in many ways and can rarely get on.
A woman may lose her heart to a man, while he only loses
money.

He will call her a broad, a chick or a bird.
While she calls him honey.

He will say `baby you look ravishing tonight; I like your
hairdo'.
While she says `oh I love your shirt, the colour suits you'.

Ask me what I think?
I'm still thinking about it.

The Poor Man

Depression, frustration, and a whole lot of meditation.
Often lead up to a slow, heavy vexation.
Makes me wonder, am I alive?
In this world of today, its' one hell of a struggle just trying to
survive.

World crises, inflation, and the present economic situation.
Creates within an almost violent, and suicidal intention.
Where is the poor man's chance?
Is he just passed off with an insignificant glance?

Yet amid the rapid changes of this vast complicated world.
The poor man has the right to eat, strive, and exist.
Even though prices take a hike and things may go amiss.

Who is the poor man?
Where is the poor man?
In my estimation, I am the poor man…
And many more like me, who just can't understand.

[Dedicated to my sister]

Lazy Girl.

Lazy, very hazy, almost deprived, and crazy.
This child of radiant youth possesses only the power to sleep
and loot,
always arising in time for grub and bickle,
demanding all, leaving nothing, regardless of how little.

Thoughtless of infant's need to protect and feed,
all must fend for themselves, she said.
I have the most incurable and ravenous greed.'

She wants all, she doesn't care
whether it be cheap or very dear.
Life goes on in just one way,
eat sleep and live for another day.

Yet days will come she'll all be worn,
a woman then quite fully grown.
No longer to think of herself alone,
but for many little children she'll call her own.

The Mind

The mind is like another planet bubbling with life and
creativity.
Thinking, scheming, alive even in sleep, I often wonder of its'
longevity.

Many high places, men reach and greatness, were just
inventive thoughts activated by 'the 'MIND'; yet following
thus can also lead to destruction, if one is weak enough to be
so inclined.

The voices of the mind are like story- tellers, speaking in
different languages and sounds. Each trying to contradict the
other, trying to win, to gain recognition, preference; a thought
used.

Priceless, mysterious, irreplaceable, and great, the mind's
capability excels above all, you're nought without it, probably
dead, but if used properly it could save you instead.

"THE MIND" the most precious gift bestowed from the
creator to mankind.

The Day My Father Died

The day my father died I felt relief.
Looking at him lifeless on the bed,
no tears, no pain, no grief, just relief.

He will 'beat' mama no more I thought.
No battering, no scream, no shout.
To me, he did the best thing, took the easy way out.

Mama cried and held her heart, for the man who abused her,
used her as a tool.
Kept her a prisoner in herself.
I thought she was a fool.

In the morgue I saw him stiff and cold,
waiting to be dressed.
I looked at his face, touched his hand,
then suddenly my heart did something wild!

I suddenly realised that whatever this man did, that I was still
his child.
I can still see him in my mind today.
And wish he hadn't died.

The President's Dilemma

So, what if the President had an affair?
Doesn't every other married man have one?
Why must he be looked upon in distaste?
Be assessed in haste, and obviously being pushed out of his place?

After all he's just a man?
Is there anything such as a perfect one?
Why the talk of isolation, degradation, and such open humiliation?
He's the President yes; we all know that.
Does that mean he's an icon and can do no wrong?

He's under a lot of pressure doing his best, even for you who oppress him.
So, give him a chance, leave him alone.
He knows what he did or did not do.
Things could have been different…it could have been you

The Clinic Scene

Mothers arriving, mothers going, looking alert, alive, and well.
Some in early stages, others advanced in pregnancy you can
tell.
Faces of anger, anticipation, and joy.
Laughing, chatting doing things they enjoy.

Doctors and nurses moving about; calling individuals,
sometimes with a shout.
Orderlies lingering for something to do, number one! number
ten!
Hesitant mothers slowly rising, answering names again and
again.

Visiting the clinic for them is secure.
Avoiding diseases, health hazards and more.
The future men and women to take our place,
are cared for by mothers in this early stage.

The clinic is great for them in this time.
For the children they bring will surely be fine.

A Smile

A smile is such a funny thing,
it goes around the world.
You smile at me,
I smile at you,
and so, one smile makes two.

A smile is such a funny thing,
you never know it's hiding place.
The only time you know it's there,
is when it wrinkles up your face.

A smile should be an everlasting thing,
but some can't keep it there,
because when you get sad and if you cry,
it suddenly disappears.

Smiling is healthy and it's fun,
it says a lot about your feelings.
Though many smile, but for a while,
you never know it's meaning.

Christiana Heart

In Manchester at one of the coolest parts,
lies this dear little place only known as 'Heart.'
It improves the mind, put you in line
Get you ready to face the onward time.

Such a positive way to make a start
If only you appreciate and digest the interest at 'Heart.'
It starts you small, an academy for all, if training not
neglected.
It will be the beauty of life reflected.

The surroundings are great, the food is divine,
Hospitality and sanitation are at top of the line.
The discipline is tight, but if ambitious it will be your delight.
keep your cool at Christiana Heart, for priceless knowledge
they do impart.

Almost Wasted

I feel like I am drowning and have nothing to hold onto.
Not an empty boot a-floating, not a wanderer I see.
Not even a lonely car or truck tyre, around to rescue me.

Is it my sinking, dying heart, crying out for help?
Why is there no one else here, only me, all by myself?
I'm trying to scream, no words will come, I'm losing all my breath.
I want to shout, to see someone, to pray before my death.

My hands are flailing in the air, as the water pulls me down.
I'm kicking wildly, struggling still, am I really going to drown?
My heart is beating fast! I can feel it in my head!
I guess this is how you really feel, before you are truly dead.

Where is my life? What have I done for a punishment so hard?
Oh, tell me now before I go, is this my destiny Lord?
I'm gasping Lord, I'm begging you, is this the result of my sin?
Stretch out your hand and rescue me, my head is going in.

Slowly but surely, I feel it, someone is lifting me.
I know it's you sweet Lord, for it can only be done by thee.
You have spared my life and given me wings, to await my coming flight.
I'm rising Lord, I'm floating now towards the utmost height.

Freedom

Imagine me without freedom?

Freedom to talk.
Freedom to express.
Freedom to move.
Freedom to live.

This is freedom!

To express my desires and expectations.

To talk of my fears, my love, my dreams.

To move, go where I please, when I want if I want.

To live anywhere in this world without obstruction and surveillance.

My brothers and sisters lived like this once, their freedom taken away by oppressors who called themselves masters. Masters who beat them, overworked them, underfed them, restricted, and imprisoned them, bound them in chains and called them slaves.

Masters who inflict, instruct, and disrupt, who were corrupt and in the end self-destruct. '

'Freedom' a God given right to all mankind, for all humans, regardless of sex, race or colour. Our freedom was bought by our forefathers and mothers, who all suffered and died to make us free.

FREEDOM! I salute you. freedom! freedom! freedom!

I am a Poet

I am a poet! I am a poet!
I don't stand on the roof top and shout it.
You may see me, talk and laugh with me and;
you wouldn't even know it.

I am a poet! I am a poet!
I see it, I feel it and so I write it.
It's about you, it's about me, it's about everything,
that I'm able to see, touch and feel.

I am a poet! I am a poet!
It's natural and real the things I say,
the things I feel, my ever-roaming thoughts;
I cannot conceal.

I am a poet! I am a poet! A black woman and proud.
I can be discreet, I can be silent, and I can be loud.
Expressing myself is what I do best.
It's just words, I'm not the best but go ahead, put me to the
test.

CHAPTER 3

JAMAICAN PATOIS (PATWA)

[This was specifically written about my ex-husband. I would observe him sitting down on the floor, knees up to his chin, smoking the weed and looking into space. Once in a while he would smile, but it wasn't with me, he was in another world]

Ganja Baby

Him a roll it, him a mek it, him a puff it, him a smoke it.
Him sid dung one place a mek up im face.
Him a laugh, him a chat to no one.

Him sey weed no bad, it mek him feel glad, yet I wonder
and I ponder why him luk so sad? Him a smile, him a chant.
Him mek mi laugh, a mussi more him want.

Di weed man, di weed, all it du, is full yu up wid greed.
Dat ting noh chek fi neither race, color nor creed.
Once yu mek it become a habit, any weh it deh, yu a fi fine it.

Or it have yu sidung eena one pose, lookin down pon
nothing but yu nose.

Mad Man

Di man a pick di grass luk eena di pan, luk up eena di sky, luk
dung pan im han, a wah dweem sah? A mus mad im mad or a
bad im bad?
Him git up a fite, him a run, him fall dung, lawd amassi pan di
grung!
Him mout a bleed but im a dance, a tear up him clothes an ah
jump an prance.

Him dutty an smell bad eh? Clothes have a t'ousan hole.
All im parts deh a doh, an him walkin like him de pon stage
show.
Man, an ooman pass him by, an pickney a goh a school; dem
noh badda troble im, cause dem know him fool.

Unoo luk yah! Him luk nice dis maanin, dress up eena him cleanest
dirty clothes.
Him blackis white cap, an roun him waise, piece a hose.
Him nevva si di caar in time, Waai! It lik him dung! Mi tink di
mad man ded!
All him do; is luk up, luk dung an Run!

[My best description of one of the usual days on a bus from the country into Kingston, back then in the 70s-90s

P for passenger

C for Conductor

D for driver]

Jamaica Bus Running

(P) A weh di bus deh sah? A how it tek so long? Seet a bus di caana deh, luk like it well, well ram. (P) One stop driva! Noh cah mi go too far, (P) 'cum dung fi di stap lady, an noh mek mi war. (P) 'Lawd sah tek yu time, noh push an shub mi soh, mi hab mi bag an sinting dem, a Kingston mi a goh.'

(P) Gu dung eena di bus an clear di way fimi, people! People! unoo def? luk how di bus empty? Tek out unoo fare an mek sure hav it rite, cause wen mi com fi calek mi caan badda wid di fite. (P) Ole aan ducta! mi tink mi lef mi purse, yu noh it drap outa mi bag, cause one a dem did burse?

(C) Si yah ooman, cum off ah di bus rite now, how come yu run fi ketch di bus, before yu luk fi dat? (P) Driva drive di bus an mek di ooman sidung! a noh di fus free drive yu a go gi smady, fi gudung eena tung? (C) Cease driva! di bus nah move anless she pay di fare, a noh waata a run dis, an even gas get dear!

(P) Mek all a wi tan ya den, an si who a go lose, if you decide fi crawl den mek wi enjoy di cruise. (D) A wanda if unoo noh mi run dis ya bus by time? (D) Unoo tink it can pay mi fi si dung pan mi behind? Try settle di war an mek di bus move aan, cause wedda unoo agree yes or no, a gaan mi gaan.

C) Come ooman pass up di money or cumout! Noh badda mek mi a fi leggo some terrible wud outa mi mout. (P) Si di money yah ooligan bwoy, tap harass di ooman now. C) Driva drive di bus! A town wi a goh, everyting reddy, cris an live!

[On my first visit to London England in 1996, I couldn't
understand the weather. I couldn't see the reason why I was
freezing, even though the sun was shining, and there wasn't
any snow]

Mi Come a London

Mi com a London, yes mi com a London; noh sno nah fall, oh
no none at all.
Di train dem nuff an di bus dem more, di people dem all
about.
Makin a shout because di sun is out; noh sno nah fall, oh no
none at all.

England is nice but wid it come a price, cause if yu walkin in
di sun an yu figat fi tek yu coat, bam! Di rain com dung, yu
nevah tek noh waanin, yu tink it was a joke. Dat nah ketch
mi, cause mi always cole, even doh no sno nah fall, oh no
none at all.

Dem sey a summa time, mi si it, but mi noh feel it, cause sun
caan a shine an yu cole like ice. It strange to mi, mi caan figga
it out, mi did hear bout it,
but pass it off as wud a mout. Mi com a London but noh fi
lang, good ting mi country mi nevva did abandon.

Now mi kno why people com a England an get fat; dem eat up
di good food an sidung one place, a watch di wedda an ah mek
up dem face. Di sun noh shine, soh dem noh swet, dem noh lose
noh energy so every ting tek set. It reely coul fi tru, mi can tell yu
dat, cause rite now it sem like even mi a get fat.

Mi com a London fi si little site see, but rite now a only one
ting a badda mi, cause wen mi go home, mi caa tell noh bady
sey, mi did si dis, mi did si dat, for even doh noh sno nah fall,

oh no, none at all, mi was jus like di rest. Mi coul mi noh go noh weh!

Heads a Government

Chat bout! Walk bout! Fly out! Bout dem a sort out di
country's financial problem, wen di only problem is dem.

Flyin all around on poor people's taxes, livin in big hotel an
relaxin; me an
you workin from mornin till night, stretchin every penny thin,
but still can't get it right.

Heads a government from all countries meet, skin dem teet,
an tek dem seat;
sidung eena di house, a knock table an ah shout, bout a poor
people welfare dem a look bout.

Heads a government mi foot! Wid dem diplomatic speech,
big pile a paper, ice water an symphathetic look; a who dem a
fool? Nowadays everybody go a school! Dem a crook!

People still hungry, naked, sick and dying, noh have a decent
house; an is not because wi not tryin.. Di money weh dem get
fi help wi, dem join
syndicate an fatten dem pocket, an di main purpose dem figat
it!

Yet come election time, dem fight fi di seat; tell lie pan dem
one anedda, an practice deceit. Dem noh have noh solution!
Only worldwide pollution an destruction! Cause if dem have
di ansa, how come wi still a suffa?

[Many of you might remember Hurricane Gilbert in 1988, it was a very frightening experience for me and my children. This is my personal description of it]

Hurricane Gilbert

Gilbert? Yes dem sey it a come an Gilbert is di name.
So tie up, pack up yu importants mek sure, cause wen Gilbert strike yu might noh hav noh more.

Tidey Monday? yes mi dear espec im around two, wen im reach an tart tear dung, a weh wi a go do? Wi mite a fi hide wi mite a fi run, all yu do eena yu hase tek care noh tumble dung.

Mi a fi si it aldoh mi friten bad, di lilly pickney dem a jump an shout a talk bout how dem glad, poor ting dem a pity dem no noh dat if dis yah Gilbert shuda blow di ole a dem lef outa doh.

Yes Honourable Gilbert di seventh in di season, come dis time at last widout cause or reason, it mite change wi life style or even mek it pwile, all mi a beg is dat it spare mi an mi chile.

Di breeze a get ruff an di rain deh pan wi, baps! di tree limb brok, bak fut miss Matty house blow weh, move deh gimi pass mek mi luk out an si Gilbert, but a wah dis reely a gwan upon di face a di eart?

Some a bawl, some unda table some quinge up eena caana, mi pray silent eena mi hart unda di bed beside Laana. Hear she depon a wispa "Lord spare me, I'm so young not ready to die" mi bus outa laff beside har aldoh mi did reely wan fi cry.

Di house a tretch like elastic, lawd! di top fly off, di pickney
dem a wet up waai hear dem tart a cough, all mass Zacky zinc
dem gone buff! Buff! all di tree dem a drop some eena mi
crap a caan.

Gilbert ease up, mi luk outa doh, six hour gone now faba like
im tap blow, mi ole up mi han, tank God im save mi life.
Gilbert 88? Wi mus memba im nevva nice.

[My elder son graduated from school in 1997 and was just contented to stay home and sleep until 12 or 1pm in the afternoons, then get up and scavenged for food. After his 18th birthday, I noticed he wasn't in any hurry to go out and find a job, things were hard in Jamaica then, I was a lone mother, I needed help. I got up one morning, looked at him sleeping, and just wrote this poem I showed him many years later, he denied he was ever like that]

Lazy Boy

Bwoy git up outa di bed, tap lidung an a gwaan like yu ded,
Go eena di bachume, taste di tootpaste, dash wata pan yu face.
Put aan yu clothes, tie yu shoelace.

Mi bring yu up all alone wid sufferin tears.
No daddy, no husband, no man to care.
Goh fine wok, use yu mout, ask aroun, yu yung an trang.
Tighten yu belt! Comb yu hair! Run along!

Life noh easy, mi sure yu know.
Mi a tell yu dat from yu a pickney a grow.
Yu a bi man now, yu a fi goh out deh.
Tek di bull by di haan as dem seh.

Mi a yu madda bwoy, noh tink seh mi haad.
But yu need fi get out ah di yaad.
Goh out deh! Step bold! Be a man!
Tek yu place in di worl weh yu belong.

Bills fi pay, food afi eat.
Yu need money ina yu packit fi goh a street.
Yu have good edication an andastandin.
Put it to use bwoy! Stop skylarkin!

60

[This one sum up most of my struggles as an illegal, lone mother trying to cope in a place without help, without any one to look out for me. It was just me, my children God and the System]

Life eena Ingland

Ten years a strife, cudnt get anyweh wid mi life, hardship and struggle, fighting as if mi going to war!

All ah ten years a mi life.

The govament system, the system, the system, dats all mi hear bout, the system. dem pull you een tight and let yu go like a sling shot, dem queeze an push yu eena caana, dem noh care if yu crawl like a iguana lizard, wedda it sunny, it rainy or a blastid blizzard.

All ah ten years a mi life.

Wen mi come ya fus, mi wudda walk round di block ova and ova jus lukin for a kind face fi beg 50p, jus need it fi mek porridge fi mi son, mi baby, mi likkle pickney…mi buk up wan man…him ask mi weh yu afi gimmi?..mi sey fi 50p? him sey nutten fi nutten…lawd mi si di vision ah miself buryin mi son, him ded fi hungrey!…go wid smady? fi 50p? afta ah noh man mi want?

All ah ten years a mi life.

Yes, sah it ruff yah soh, mi can rite a book, a noh ugly mi ugly, a noh illiterate needah but if yu noh hav weh di system want, mite as well yu live eena housetop like a spida. No mercy, no love, noh, compassion fi di run weh illegal, di abscunda as dem call yu…as far as dem concern wi is no baddy.

All ah ten years a mi life.

Mi kno every district eena Birmingham, mi almost move every month, mi caa open removal business believe mi, mi sure kno how fi pack! if ah cawd bode bax an black bag yu want…check mi, mi know weh fi find dat. dem hav mi all ova di place, wen mi tink a piece an safety an time fi settle dung, baps! ah only time fi move again, mi still de pon di move

All ah ten years ah mi life.

But God prevail, im good to mi, mi ovacome di worse, dem try fi beat mi down, mi almost en up eena hurse. Mi motto is nevah giv up, stan firm an strang, even eena di face a persecution. A Gad wi serve, all di tings weh man gwaan wid, im noh treat wi as we deserve. Mi a livin proof, cause mi get stroke, was homeless wid a chile fi tek care of, but guees wah? Mi still deh ya. Giv praise to Jah!

Memory Lane Back a Yaad

You know sometimes yu jus chillin an tryin not to focus on any ting special, an baps! a sudden memory jus tek yu? well dats wat happen 2me jus now...an mi sey mek mi talk bout it.

Mi memba wen wi live inna di country way bak den, an the family poor like chuch mouse, living way below di poverty line, but wi did happy, wi nevva kno sey wi poor. dem time deh ppl cudnt buy (decent crockery plates an cups) wi afi use enamel mug an plastic. plastic plate, plastic cup, plastic bowl, only the pot yu put pon fire a nevah plastic, woooi. wen yu luk pon di mug dem, dem chippy chippy an sometime dem leak, anyway mi best memory is about di plastic plate.

Fimi madda did have some yellow, green and red ones and cups to match, an wen she cook di curry chicken back, the greasy yellow ile (oil) stick to di plastic, yu afi use hot wata an plenty soap fi get it out. most times we nevva hav noh soap, so wi go pick susumba bush or grass an rub it up till it sud, an wash di plate. mi massy oh! ah dat time it greasy, it look same way, it smell same way, but well wash an tun dung...waiting fi di adda meal...even sometime yu use di bush wash it...the green mix wid the yellow turn it orange, mi mumma! but dat was our life, wi didn get stress ovah greasy smelly plates...wi jus wait til soap come along maybe one or two weeks after...(an it wasn't dish washing liquid either!) jus some soap powder or cake soap.

sometime wi afi luk bak, how far wi come, how much wi hav now...it's like jumping from di water Gully straight into the Atlantic Ocean...but wi tek it fi granted. wi need to be thankful...BLESSINGS!

CHAPTER 4

PROSE

I am the story

This is a poem, this is a tale, this is my story, this is a collection of words, news and views, I am Leonie and I am the story.

There was a girl born and raised in deep countryside; rivers and streams run by, ducks and ducklings flapped their wings and swam as I carried my heavy water bucket, full to the brim, so mother could wash and cook and sing; though poor as hell, she raised me well, this I can tell, this girl is me, I am the story.

Looking back now, it all seemed hard, had to bend realyl low to sweep the yard, no standing broom then…as I have now, then off to the fields I'd go to pick chocolate pods, gather coconuts and plum… a new age now, new body, new look, this is me, the same inside, hard to believe, but I am the story.

Life crisis, death and pain I've suffered that, many tears have run, many things I've done, some of it was certainly not fun; life has been good, and has been bad, I've laughed a lot and have been sad. Taking a peek back in my past now, it's been a complex but awesome journey, and all because I am the story.

My story is the truth, my story is alive as I am, I live in it, I am it, many people come and go in my story; some with a smile, some idled for a while, some brought advice, some even seemed wise, but no matter who they were, they leave and I am left alone in my story, because I am the story.

The Child in Me

The child in me yearns for green fields with rich soil, yielding sweet juicy mangos, sour sops, june plums, jack fruit, pink grapefruit, guavas and endless fruits to satisfy my insatiable appetite.

The child in me yearns for early mornings, waking up to the colourful sunrise, listening to the birds chirp their merry songs as if to say; "Good morning!" watching our masterful striped feathered rooster, standing on legs of iron and crows as if his life depended on it.

The child in me yearn for my mother's Johnny cakes and saltfish, washed down with hot vanilla chocolate, swinging my foot on the bamboo bench in the kitchen, listening to my mother sing as she works and thinking, 'this is the best!' 'Life can't get any better than this?!

The child in me long to run to school barefooted with school bag on my back, carrying books for four, yes four of us children, with twenty cents in my pocket, for our lunch which provided enough. I was the oldest, they listened to me, did what I said. Couldn't wait for the school to be over, so I could run home for my mama's red peas soup with salt beef and pig foot, as my daddy was a pig farmer, among many other things…yes, I miss those days.

The child in me long to run behind the water truck as it came round, with my plastic bucket trying to take as much as I could, run behind the sprinkler and the tar truck, sticking stones to my heels, pretending I was wearing spike. Yes, I ran behind anything with wheels. My brother's home-made skate was a thrill but climbing trees on ladders with slingshots made of sticks and rubber bands to shoot the nearest bird, was my favourite. Did I shoot one? Can't remember.

Yes, if I could repeat those days when I lived below the poverty line and didn't know it. We had everything we needed. I loved it. I was happy enjoying the naturalness of life away from this new complicated world, without televisions, mobile phones, refrigerators, electric stoves, electric light, electric irons, kettles, you name it. I was safe I want to feel this again. The CHILD in me CRIES!!

Moving Here
(Me and UK Immigration in the year 2000)

The flight coming over was a smooth and easy one, but that's where the niceness ended for me when I came here in 2000. I never knew if I got into terminal four or five, all I know is that I thanked God I was still alive.

The airport looked strange, I saw people of all different colours, everything looked shiny and glistening. "Is this your first visit mam?" repeated the voice. 'No, 'second' I said, and then realised I wasn't listening. 'Mi head gaan bak a jamaica'

"Go si yu eena Inglan tomorrow, penetrated my sister's voice back at the airport in Jamaica; send some a di trang pound fi mi." "Lawd God help mi", mi pray, as mi step up eena di line at immigration. Mi start feel nervous, foot them get weak, heart tumping cause mi nevah like di luk a di man.

Mi never si a man like dis before, the English man look weird; orange eye lash, ginger hair, freckled face and a little brown bush, I guess im call a beard. Poor me standing there, passport in mi hand tryin to figure out this man, predicting my own future while trying to control mi shaking hand. Im tek mi book an wid one luk said, "mam have a seat I'll be roight beck".

After sitting out what seemed like months, he called me to a room, the questions he began to ask was nothing short of rude; questions like: did you buy your ticket or was it sent? Why would your cousin buy such an expensive ticket for just a few months? Have you got a love interest here mam? I gasped! Hesitated and lingered over most of his questions, this man was really crude!

Two big burly men looking like weightlifters came in and took my bags, and they began to search. Dem dig and squeeze and tear, even knocking on the heels of my shoes; they acted as if I wasn't even there, I felt so abused.

"What's the purpose of this?" I asked. "Just procedure mam, just procedure", was the calm reply. A female came in and did her bit with her body search, going where no woman should, I felt sure I was going to die.

After trying his utmost best to find me in the wrong, he seemed almost disappointed to tell me "mam you can now move along". He stamped my book and pushed it towards me with that expressionless, robotic look and as if with a recorded voice; said, "Enjoy your stay mam"

The Cheek!

CHAPTER 5

FAITH

Pleading Heart

Lord I come to you faint, miserable and broken.
With all my thoughts scrambled, tangled and unspoken.
The heavy burdens I bear in this world of care.
Oh, dear Lord, I want you near.

I need your presence Lord, can't go through this without you.
More than ever, I need your guidance in all I do.
Dear Lord, the world is spinning out of control.
Your shining glory and loving face, I long to behold!

Oh, come now Lord, tarry no longer, lest I die?
I am your child, not holy but Lord I try.
Your promises are true, your will is pure.
I want to inherit that golden kingdom forevermore.

Please hear me Lord I plead with thee!
Keep me safe and stand by me.
While the shadows of death are closing in.
Grant me sweet peace and blot out my sin.

Thank you, Lord!

My Prayer

Father why is my life headed for the drain?
And why must I be enduring all this pain?
My life is precious, this I know.
Please give me my chance and let me go.

I've yearned for freedom all my life, just
Grant me this one wish and remove the strife.
I'm always being pushed in the wrong direction.
Dear God, give me your protection.

I've been your child from my mother's womb.
You stood by me from morn till noon.
I trust you lord, you are my guide,
I know you'll always be by my side.

I've lived my life almost in vain.
I tried so hard, but nothing gained.
I can't go on I must rebel.
This course of life I cannot dwell.

I must move, I must make haste.
To put an end to these wasted days.
Oh, protect me lord I ask of you.
Whatever you say I'll gladly do.

Direct my path I ask you lord.
Stand up for me and plead my cause.
My earthly reign shall be in vain.
If from me, you should refrain.

Amen.

Loving you Lord

I want to ever love you Lord, oh my Savior, because you are
love.
You gave us the commandment to love as you love.
Help us each day to watch and pray, to look towards your
heavenly glory.
When you shall come to claim us as your own.

I worship only you Lord; you are worthy of my praise.
You are the God of ancient days,
you are the God of now.
To you only Lord will I ever bow.

Help me to always keep a song in my heart, and praise upon
my lips.
Teach me your truths, open my eyes to see you as you are!
My Father, my sustainer, my everlasting Redeemer.
I love you Lord, stay with me till the end.

Amen.

The Almighty Father.

Give Him praise! Give Him praise! The everlasting Father, the King of Heaven and Ruler of earth. Praise him for all the many wondrous works He has done in our lives, His saving grace, His divine love.

I cry to you Lord in my time of need, and when I could not see the way, you heard, you listened, then said; 'my child your sins be forgiven thee, go in peace and wait on me.'

I thank you Lord, you are my guiding light, you keep me going through day and night. Without your love I could not stand, oh Lord my God, you understand. My heart swells with gratitude and praise, help me to serve you for the rest of my days.

Amen

The End

Printed in Great Britain
by Amazon